MOSES MALONE

by GARY LIBMAN

C Creative Education

Published by Creative Education, 123 South Broad Street, Mankato, Minnesota 56001.

Library of Congress Number: 83-71576   ISBN: 0-89813-120-0

In some ways Moses Malone is ordinary. His favorite entertainments are video games, movies, and dining in restaurants. He walks awkwardly, his arms, legs and head moving at slightly different paces.

Yet there are ways in which no 6-foot-10, 255-pound man can be ordinary. That is especially true for Moses.

Moses won the National Basketball Association's Most Valuable Player award twice and the offensive rebounding championship three times while he played for Houston. Many people think he is the best player in the world.

Before the 1982-1983 season, Houston traded him to Philadelphia where he signed a $13.2 million contract for six years. He became the highest paid team athlete in the world.

Malone was expected to lead Philadelphia to a world championship, an achievement which escaped Moses in Houston. The championship also had escaped outstanding Philadelphia teams for the six years before he arrived.

That was another challenge for Moses who has made a career of overcoming them. He was the first player in 26 years to go from high school to the major leagues of professional basketball. Out of Petersburg, Virginia, High School he signed to play with the Utah Stars of the American Basketball Association.

Now Moses needed to prove he could play with men much older and more experienced. When the American Basketball Association (ABA) went out of business, Moses moved to the older, more established National Basketball Association (NBA). He had done well in the ABA, but people thought he had played against weak opposition.

He proved himself by starring in a slow, controlled offense at Houston.

Moses as a high school basketball sensation, shows his reach to the delight of Utah Stars owner James A. Collier in New York. Malone at 19 signed a lucrative long-term contract with the Stars.

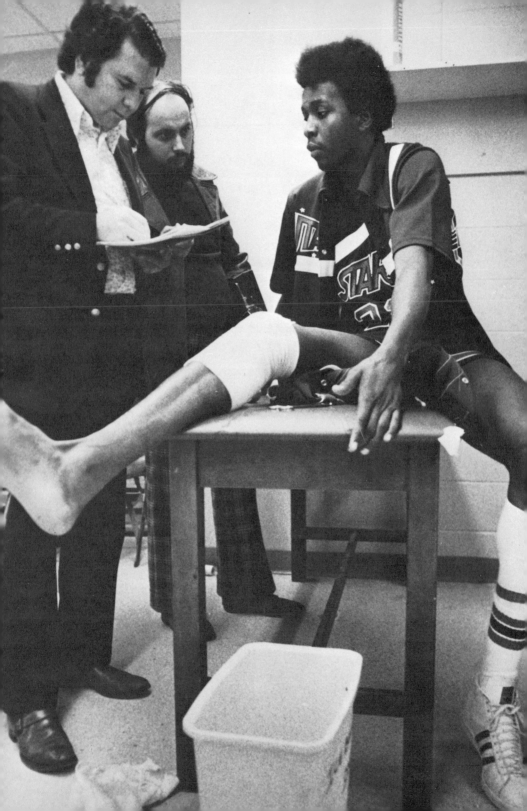

When he was traded to Philadelphia, experts said he had to prove he could run and pass to fit into their offense. He was successful almost overnight, perhaps because hard work has always been a part of his game.

Moses' specialty, rebounding, demands more work than any other part of basketball.

In rebounding the player grabs the ball when it bounces off the rim or backboard after a miss. Under the rim is the most crowded area on the basketball court. A lot of bumping, elbowing, and shoving goes on there.

To get the ball Moses has to be ready to take and give that kind of punishment. And he has to want the ball badly.

A long time ago Moses started figuring out how to be the best rebounder possible.

Today Moses studies each player to determine whether he shoots a flat, hard shot or a soft arching one. Then Moses can predict where the ball will most likely go if it doesn't go through the basket.

He knows his teammates best, and he knows that most good shooters will miss to the side of the rim away from them.

When a shot goes up, Moses instantly determines where the ball will bounce if it's a miss. Then he moves there, fast.

Moses' rebound efforts make his team hard to beat if a game is close in the last quarter. By then, after fighting him all night, many opponents are fatigued. Moses isn't. When he senses his opponent is weary, he moves even faster.

But even if the game isn't close or nearly over, Moses wants <u>every</u> rebound. In the NBA, where the players are the best in the world, most rebounders only try for about 20 rebounds a game and get six or seven. Moses tries for 100 to 150 and gets 20.

Moses (24) crashed into Milwaukee's Ernie Grunfeld (20) as he drives for the basket.

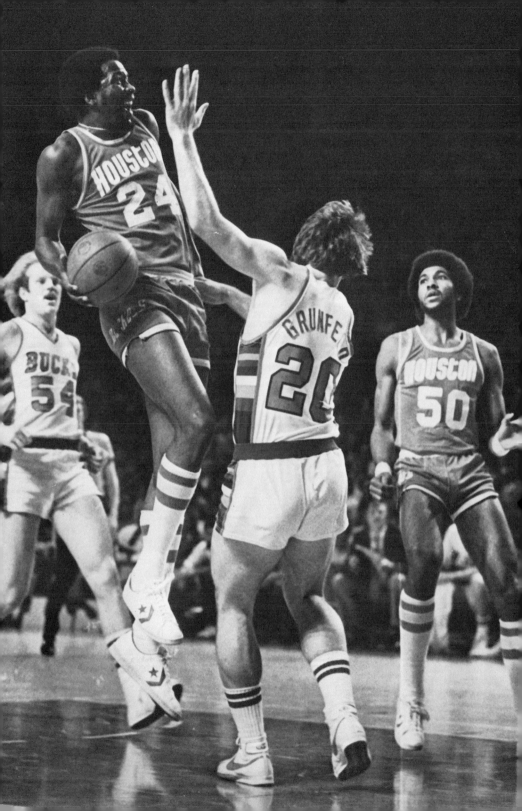

Moses is intent on making this slam dunk during a game with the Atlanta Hawks.

In addition to his study of players' shooting habits Moses is a good rebounder because he is quick and agile for his size. Moses also has great desire.

"That's where you start when you discuss Moses—his overwhelming desire," one professional coach comments, as he compares Moses to two other great rebounders. "Neither of them wanted the ball as badly as Moses does."

Moses always had desire. In high school in Petersburg, Virginia, where he was already 6-foot-10, Moses led his team to a 50-0 record and two state championships his last two years.

He had grown up in an old house that seemed to be falling apart. The plumbing often failed and there was a hole where there should have been a window.

His mother supported Moses, an only child, on $100 a week she earned at a local supermarket. Moses' father left long before, when Moses was two years old.

Moses' mother, Mary, had been poor all her life. She wanted something more for Moses. She made sure Moses didn't have to work. So he played basketball instead.

Moses was about 14 when he began to realize how good a basketball player he really was.

He wrote a message to himself and placed it in the worn family Bible. To this day, Moses doesn't talk much about the message, but people close to Moses know what he wrote. Apparently he promised himself to become the best high school basketball player in the country by his junior year.

Later he wrote another note, this time promising to become the first high school player to go directly to professional basketball.

Moses was such a good high school player that 300 college coaches wanted him. For many athletes, college provides an education and the training for a job after graduation. Colleges often pay for athlete's books, tuition, and living expenses. Sometimes this is the only way an athlete can afford to attend college.

Moses was so talented that he could skip college and become the one-in-a-million athlete who goes from high school to the NBA. When he found out how much money he could make there, Moses had a hard choice to make.

At first Moses planned to go to college. He signed a commitment to attend the University of Maryland.

During this time, many coaches made repeated trips to Petersburg to convince Moses to attend their school. One of them spent 61 days in town just waiting to talk to Moses.

Moses visited nearly 25 colleges. Occasionally he found them too eager.

"Sometimes they brought me in to meet the president of the university who talked to me like he wanted to be my father. That made me laugh," Moses remembers. "They fixed me up with dates. Then when I got home those girls called me long distance and pretended they were in love with me. What kind of stuff is that?"

Expecting recruiters all the time now, Moses sometimes hid when he heard a knock at the door. His friends knocked in a secret code. To get away Moses went off to play basketball without telling his mother.

Eventually Moses agreed to go to Maryland, he says, because the coach was honest.

Shortly after Moses made this commitment, the Utah Stars of the American Basketball Association began to negotiate with him. The ABA started as a rival to the older, more established NBA. It was looking for good, interesting players to attract customers and TV contracts.

Moses was a good player and his youth (no one had gone from high school to the NBA since

Moses goes high above Lakers Kareem Abdul-Jabbar, left, and Mark Landsberger for a rebound.

1948) was a natural curiosity. Could someone that young play against men so much older and more mature?

Moses said he never doubted what to do.

"I'd seen the pros on TV and I figured I was quicker," he says. "People talked about experience, but I never thought experience meant that much under the rack (basket). So I told my momma, let me decide. If I'm going to lose, let me lose myself. So my momma said all right."

Critics howled as Moses' signed. They said it deprived him of a college education, a chance to be a better person, a better citizen, and prepare for a job. Others disagreed, saying that the $3.3 million contract for five years would provide Moses with lifetime security and the chance to get a college education later, whenever he wanted.

Moses took the money and bought his mother a new home in a nice neighborhood. He also

Moses reaches in and grabs the ball from Kareem Abdul-Jabbar. Houston went on to upset the Lakers 111-107 in the first round of the 1981 NBA Western Conference Playoffs.

furnished the new house and bought his mother a car. Moses told her boss at the market that she would not be working any longer. He began sending her enough money so she could pay all her bills each month.

When Moses started to play with Utah, he was shy. Some people thought he wasn't smart enough. He was nervous about interviews, so he said little and often looked at his feet. A disc jockey in Salt Lake City nicknamed him "Mumbles." That hurt Moses.

Moses' school work was average. He substituted an art class for an algebra class so he could be sure to graduate from high school with a C average. Nevertheless, representatives in contract talks with Utah came to believe Moses is smart when he needs to be.

Moses was represented by Donald Dell, a lawyer in Washington, D.C. Their first meeting was in Dell's office. Dell says that as soon as he entered the room, Moses dropped his head.

Moses rolls the ball off fingertips for two.

"At that time," Dell remembers, "that was his natural response to any stranger. I wanted to catch his attention, and so I walked right over to him, and even before I said hello, I said, 'You ever hear of slavery, Moses?' His head came up like that. He stared straight at me, and he listened to every word I said."

Dell explained the contract Utah was offering and told Moses to feel free to call back when he needed advice. The next day, during further talks with Utah, Malone did.

"Eighteen calls—18," Dell said. "Every time Utah made a new move, Moses called me. I knew then that he was a lot smarter than he was given credit for."

Something else happened. The better the Utah offer became, the more certain it seemed that Moses was going to play professional basketball.

Late in the discussions over the Utah contract, Moses and Dell met with Maryland Coach Lefty

Moses can't be stopped by Golden State Warriors center Joe Barry Carroll.

Driesell, a very persuasive man. Driesell tried to convince Moses that God would not mind if Moses did not keep the promise he wrote in the family Bible. The coach urged Moses to wait a few years to enter professional basketball. When Moses was unconvinced, Driesell got frustrated and became emotional. Suddenly Moses looked up and glared at him. "Stop jivin' me, Coach," Moses said. And that was it. The decision was made—Moses would join Utah.

Many people thought Moses was too young to succeed in professional basketball.

"There's a 50-50 chance he'll flop," said Bob Ferry, general manager of the Washington Bullets. "There's no way this kid is a Bill Walton, or a Kareem Abdul-Jabbar, or a Wilt Chamberlain."

Tom Heinsohn, then coach of the Boston Celtics, said, "It's utterly ridiculous to pay this kind of money to a kid like this. He may be great but there's no way a 19-year-old kid is going to step into pro basketball and be great right off the bat."

Moses may not have been great, but he played well. On October 4, 1974, he scored 15 points and grabbed 13 rebounds in his first exhibition game. For his first year he averaged 18.8 points and 14.6 rebounds a game.

His coach, Tom Nissalke, helped Moses mature. Sometimes in team huddles he stopped everything, waiting until Moses raised his head to listen and to look Nissalke in the eye.

Although Moses did well his first year, Utah and the ABA went out of business the next season. The ABA couldn't sign enough talented players or build enough interest to survive against the more established NBA.

The NBA offered contracts to Moses and other top players in the ABA. Portland signed Moses, but many NBA teams questioned his value. He was still only 19, lacking a college background, said to be so very quiet. He had compiled good statistics with Utah, but some thought the competition in the ABA had been weak. And Moses' $300,000-a-year contract was big in 1976.

So Portland traded him to Buffalo, who quickly traded him to Houston. The second trade was done at the urging of Nissalke, who had moved from Utah and was now head coach at Houston.

The trade was made October 25, 1976, and it was from that date that Moses began to establish himself in the NBA.

In his last four seasons in Houston, Moses averaged 15.4 rebounds and 27.7 points per game. The team usually finished high in the standings. In 1978-79 Moses averaged 17.6 rebounds per game and got a higher percentage of his teams' rebounds than any player in NBA history.

Moses has been so good at rebounding shots missed by his teammates—offensive rebounds—

Rick Mahom (44) and Don Collins (22) of the Washington Bullets close in on Moses to stop his drive to the basket.

Newly acquired Philadelphia 76ers center Moses Malone and
team owner Harold Katz sit together during a news conference.
The 76ers acquired Malone from the Houston Rockets for
Caldwell Jones and the 1983 first round draft choice.

that Boston Celtics' president Red Auerbach has said he thinks that Moses "may well be the best offensive rebounder of all time." Auerbach coached Bill Russell, one of the all-time great centers.

Moses' former teammate at Houston, guard Calvin Murphy, goes even further. "Moses Malone is the best basketball player in the world," Murphy once said. "He can do whatever is asked of him."

Because he is so talented, Moses was very attractive to Philadelphia. Three seasons in the last six, Philadelphia had lost in the final round of championship play. Fans and team officials were getting tired of second-place finishes. They wanted a championship.

The owners thought they could pay Moses' $13.2 million by cutting other payroll expenses and by winning a championship. The win would sell more game tickets and bring in more TV money.

They believed the team could win the championship if Moses replaced an inconsistent player named Darryl Dawkins. They traded one high-salaried player to Houston to acquire Moses and let go several other expensive players, including Dawkins.

Philadelphia General Manager Pat Williams, has said that Moses ". . . is about as riskless as a sports investment as you can make. He doesn't require any special privileges. He's just one of the troops.

"Remove Darryl and plug this guy in and it's like night and day. With this guy you know what's going to happen night after night. With Darryl, you didn't know . . . from play to play."

The question most asked about Moses' arrival in Philadelphia was whether he could fit in with the team's fast-break offense. This requires Moses to rebound the ball and make a quick, hard pass to a teammate at the side of the court.

Moses gets fouled by Washington Bullets Dave Batton while going up for a two point attempt.

Then he and his teammates race to the other end of the court to score before the other team can retreat.

Although Moses had played in a different, slower system at Houston, he quickly learned to handle the Philadelphia method.

Philadelphia's Coach Billy Cunningham has said the exhibition season convinced him that Moses could do whatever was asked because he wanted to win.

"Moses will fit in any place," Calvin Murphy has observed. "Moses can throw an outlet pass (to the side of the court). He's never been asked to."

Settled in Philadelphia, Moses seems pleased with his own development.

"I don't let the pressure get to me," he says. "I don't worry about what people think about Moses. Moses is a human being. Moses ain't

Moses is guarded by Los Angeles Lakers Kurt Rambis. Harold Katz, the 76ers owner, paid $13.2 million plus bonuses for Moses to enable his team to win the 1983 NBA Championship.

perfect. I don't try to be no big shot. I don't try to say, 'Hey, my name is Moses, you should do this, you don't do that.'"

Moses, who is married, hopes to pass this attitude along to his son. Moses hopes that the boy "will do things right. He won't be no trouble boy, he'll be a real nice boy. I want him to believe in himself, so he won't be listening to what anyone says."

About his contract, Moses says, "I've been making a million dollars for a long time (with Houston). You get more things. You're more secure. You can be rich, you can be poor. Things happen bad, they happen good. I never put myself too high. I was a poor black kid in the ghetto but my mama raised me right. I just do my work."